In the News

Guided/Group Reading Notes

Grey Band

Contents

OXFORD

Introduction

Reading progression in Year 4/ Primary 5

By Year 4/Primary 5 the majority of children are developing into confident, capable readers. The focus is on continuing to build their reading fluency and their engagement with reading. Encouraging children to read widely in order to develop personal preferences, critical appreciation and comprehension is central to helping them become enthusiastic readers. Humour, adventure, suspense and identification with interesting characters and intriguing information texts all help create books children look forward to reading. They can sustain independent reading for extended periods of time but chapters and non-fiction spreads offer natural 'break points' for readers who may still find long texts challenging to read. They also create hooks to motivate the reader to want to read further.

Year 4/P5 children recognize most common words on sight. The texts at **grey band** include polysyllabic words and more complex topic based vocabulary. Explicit work on vocabulary continues to be important for improving both reading and writing. Introducing new vocabulary within meaningful contexts helps to extend children's vocabulary range. A wide range of vocabulary, sentence structures and verb tenses are used. Language play (puns, homophones, homonyms, codes, jokes, onomatopoeic words, etc.) can also be found in the texts. Expressive, descriptive and figurative language and vocabulary help create moods and emotions.

In the fiction books, storylines are more complex. Stories are not merely straightforward recounts, but demand inference, deduction and synthesizing of information.

The non-fiction books offer examples of a wide range of genres. There are opportunities to compare and contrast these different genres and to examine the features of each genre closely.

2

Visual literacy is supported through the range of visual 'genres' used in the books, for example, comic strips, photo sequences, diagrammatic 'animations'. At grey band, the ratio of text to illustrations/photographs is greater, but the illustrations continue to provide additional information and interest for the reader, including opportunities to compare and contrast visual information and source materials. Photos and illustrations add to the content and level of reading challenge, rather than simply supporting the text. Visualization comprehension strategies and activities that encourage the reader to reflect on the visual images are suggested in these *Guided/Group Reading Notes*.

Progression in the Project X character books

In this cluster, the gang are invited for an interview at WOW! magazine. At the same time the famous author K J Sparkling is given the 'WOW! Award for being Wonderful', but unknown to the editor-in-chief, an impostor appears (who turns out to be Dr X's mum) to try to steal the children's watches. Max's mum saves the day by capturing Mrs X who tries to escape over the roof. The real K J Sparkling claims the award and promises to use the four children as characters in her next book!

Guided/Group Reading

By Year 4/P5, guided/group reading sessions offer opportunities for children to read independently in a focused way and take part in group discussion to enhance understanding, personal response and an appreciation of the author's craft, rather than concentrating on rehearsing and applying reading cues – although there may be occasions when revisiting these is useful.

These *Guided/Group Reading Notes* provide support for each book in the cluster, along with suggestions for follow-up activities. Books in grey band can be covered in around three guided/group reading sessions. Alternatively, children may read much of each book in grey band independently and only undertake one guided/group reading session around the text. Although guided/group reading suggestions for all of the book are given under each section of the notes, teachers will select which chapters/non-fiction sections they wish to use in reading sessions.

Speaking, listening and drama

Talk continues to be crucial to learning at this stage. At Year 4/P5, children still need plenty of opportunities to express their ideas through talk and drama and to listen to and watch the ideas of others. These processes are important for building reading engagement, personal response and understanding, and for rehearsing some writing possibilities. Suggestions for speaking, listening and drama are provided for every book. Within these *Guided/Group Reading Notes* the speaking and listening activities are linked to the reading assessment focuses.

Building comprehension

Understanding what we have read is at the heart of reading.

To help readers become effective in comprehending a text these *Guided/Group Reading Notes* contain practical strategies to develop the following important aspects of comprehension:

- Previewing
- Predicting
- Activating and building prior knowledge
- Questioning
- Recalling
- Visualizing and other sensory responses
- Deducing, inferring and drawing conclusions
- Determining importance
- Synthesizing
- Empathizing
- Summarizing
- Personal response, including adopting a critical stance

The research basis and rationale for focusing on these aspects of comprehension is given in the *Teaching Handbook* for Year 4/P5.

Reading fluency

Reading fluency combines automatic word recognition and reading with pace and expression. Rereading, fluency and building comprehension are linked together in a complex interrelationship, where each supports the other. This is discussed more fully in the *Teaching Handbook* for Year 4/P5. Opportunities for children to read aloud are important in building fluency and reading aloud to children provides models of expressive fluent reading. Suggestions for purposeful and enjoyable oral reading and rereading/relistening activities are given in the follow-up activities in these *Guided/Group Reading Notes* and in the notes for parents on the inside cover of each book.

The Project X *Interactive Stories* software can be used to provide a model of reading fluency for the whole class and/or opportunities for individuals or small groups of children to listen to stories again and again. Listening to stories being read is particularly effective with EAL children.

Building vocabulary

Explicit work on enriching vocabulary is important in building reading fluency and comprehension. Repeatedly encountering a word and its variants helps it become known on sight. The thematic 'cluster' structure of Project X supports this because words are repeated within and across the books. Suggestions for vocabulary work are included in these notes. The vocabulary chart on pages 10–11 shows when vocabulary is repeated and new words are introduced. It also indicates those words that can be used to support learning alongside a structured phonics and spelling programme.

Developing a thematic approach

Helping children make links in their learning supports their development as learners. All the books in this cluster focus on the theme **In the News**. A chart showing the cross-curricular potential of this theme and further reading suggestions are given in the *Teaching Handbook* for Year 4/P5, along with a rationale for using thematic approaches. Some suggestions for cross-curricular activities are also given in these *Guided/Group Reading Notes*, in the follow-up activities suggestions for each book.

In guided/group reading sessions, you will also want to encourage children to make links between the books in the cluster. Grouping books in a cluster allows readers to make links between characters, events and actions across the books. This enables readers to gradually build complex understandings of characters, to give reasons why things happen and how characters may change and develop. It can help them recognize cause and effect. It helps children reflect on the skill of determining importance, as a minor incident or detail in one book may prove to have greater significance when considered across several books.

Note that the books in this cluster can be read in any order.

In the **In the News** cluster, some of the suggested links that can be explored across the books include:

- producing a comic strip of the important events in a story **Literacy)**
- exploring the history of newspapers and magazines (**History**)
- writing science reports for a class magazine (**Science**)
- investigating Internet newspapers. (**ICT**)

Reading into writing

The Project X books provide both writing models and inspiration to support children's writing. Brief suggestions for relevant, contextualized and interesting writing activities are given in the follow-up activities for each book. These include both short and longer writing opportunities. The activities cover a wide range of writing contexts so writers can develop an understanding of adapting their writing for different audiences and purposes.

The Project X *Interactive Stories* software contains a collection of 'clip art' assets from the character books that children can use in their writing.

Selecting follow-up activities

These *Guided/Group Reading Notes* give many ideas for follow-up activities. Some of these can be completed within the reading session. Some are longer activities that will need to be worked on over time. You should select those activities that are most appropriate for your pupils. It is not expected that you would complete all the suggested activities.

Home/school reading

Books used in a guided/group reading session can also be used in home/school reading programmes.

Before a guided/group reading session, the child could:
- read the first chapter or section of a book
- read a related book from the cluster to build background knowledge.

Following a guided/group reading session, the child could:
- reread the book at home to build reading confidence and fluency
- read the next chapter in a longer book
- read a related book from the cluster.

Advice for parents on supporting their child in reading at home is provided in the inside covers of individual books. There is further advice for teachers concerning home/school reading partnerships in the *Teaching Handbook* for Year 4/P5.

Assessment

During guided/group reading, teachers make ongoing assessments of individuals and of the group. Reading targets are indicated for each book and you should assess against these. Select just one or two targets at a time as the focus for the group. The same target can be appropriate for several literacy sessions or over several texts.

Readers should be encouraged to self-assess and peer-assess against the target/s.

Further support for assessing pupils' progress is provided in the *Teaching Handbook* for Year 4/P5.

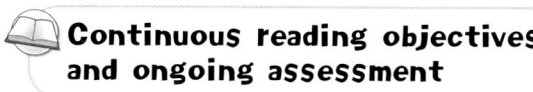
Continuous reading objectives and ongoing assessment

The following objective will be supported in *every* guided/group reading session and is therefore a continuous focus for attention and assessment (AF3). This objective is not repeated in full in each set of notes, but as you listen to individual children discussing their reading you should undertake ongoing assessment against this objective:

- Interrogate texts to deepen and clarify understanding and response **8.2**

Further framework objectives are provided as a focus within the notes for each book.

Correlation to the specific objectives within the Scottish, Welsh and Northern Ireland curricula are provided in the *Teaching Handbook* for Year 4/P5.

Recording assessment

The assessment chart for the **In the News** cluster is provided in the *Teaching Handbook* for Year 4/P5.

Diagnostic assessment

If an individual child is failing to make good progress or he or she seems to have a specific problem with some aspect of reading you will want to undertake a more detailed assessment. Details of how to use running records for diagnostic assessment are given in the *Teaching Handbook* for Year 4/P5.

 **Vocabulary chart**

At Year 4/P5, children should:

- read most words independently and automatically
- distinguish the spelling and meaning of common homophones
- know and apply common spelling rules
- develop a range of personal strategies for learning new and irregular words.

NB Examples only are given in each category.

The **WOW!** Award	Homophones	meet, seen, saw
	Spelling rule: Double consonants	disappeared, interrupted, arriving, announced, impressed, buzzed
	New and irregular context words	respected, custody, investigation, department, magazine, celebrity, successful, ceremony
WOW! Special Edition	Homophones	tail, practise
	Spelling rule: Compound words	deckchairs, undercover, blueberries, strawberries
	New and irregular context words	eco warrior, electromagnets, strolled, daydreaming, thoroughly, misunderstood, recycle, chimes, deckchairs, permission, canteen, sandwiches, undercover, emperor, blueberries, strawberries

Micro Man Makes Big News	Homophones	compliment, patience
	Spelling rule: Adding 'ed'	balanced, insured, involved, inhaled, received, privileged, struggled, decided, thinned, relieved
	New and irregular context words	journalist, exhibition, micro-sculptor, Statue of Liberty, privileged, dyslexia, scattered, shards, startlingly, microsurgeons, escapism, inspiration, colossal, underestimate, debate, insured, interview, Martin Luther King, MBE, meditation, nervous system, review, recount
The Big Story	Homophones	practise, too
	Spelling rule: Suffixes	-ly: sarcastically, bluntly, regretfully, immediately, frantically
	New and irregular context words	Gazette, headlines, cryptosporidosis, editor, freestyle, puncture, disappointment, moustache, backpack, fraud
Making a Splash	Homophones	whale, tail
	Spelling rule: Investigate and explore different long vowel phonemes	headline, Parliament, specializes
	New and irregular context words	conservationist, correspondent, dehydrated, editor, eyewitness, headline, instinct, marine mammal, news agency, plankton, printing press, publish, reporter, sonar, National History Museum, bottle-nose whale, plankton, Parliament, specializes

The WOW! Award

BY CHRIS POWLING

About this book

In this story the children have been invited to WOW! magazine to be interviewed. Here they come across several new characters including the famous author K J Sparkling. But there is more to the author than meets the eye and this leads to an exciting rooftop struggle.

You will need

- *Vocabulary detectives* Photocopy Master, *Teaching Handbook* for Year 4/P5
- *Dr X and Mrs X said ...* Photocopy Master, *Teaching Handbook* for Year 4/P5
- *Comic strip writing frame* Photocopy Master, *Teaching Handbook* for Year 4/P5

	Literacy Framework objective	Target and assessment focus
Speaking, listening, group interaction and drama	○ Offer reasons and evidence for their views, considering alternative opinions 1.1	○ We can reflect on ideas that people contribute to a discussion **AF3**
Reading	○ Identify and summarize evidence from a text to support a hypothesis 7.1 ○ Deduce characters' reasons for behaviour from their actions 7.2 ○ Interrogate texts to deepen and clarify understanding and response 8.2	○ We can identify clues to a character's personality and feelings and justify our ideas with evidence from the text **AF2/3** ○ We can answer questions and discuss what we have read **AF2/3**

The following notes provide a structure for up to three guided/group reading sessions. They are intended to be used flexibly; you may choose to focus on all three sessions or you could focus on one session and have the children read the rest of the book independently. In Session 1, children will read Chapters 1–3. In Session 2, they will read Chapters 4–6. In Session 3, children will read Chapters 7–8.

Session 1 (Chapters 1–3)

 Before reading

To activate prior knowledge and encourage prediction

- Focus on the front cover. What do the children know about award ceremonies? Why are they held? What might the award be about? Who do the children think might be receiving an award and why? Encourage children to justify their opinions with reference to previous stories. (**activating prior knowledge, predicting**)

To engage readers and support fluent reading

- Look at pages 2–3 together. What do the children notice about the genre of these pages? Is this what they were expecting? (**activating prior knowledge**)
- Ask children to check through the rest of the book – is it all in a newspaper format? Read pages 2–3 to the children. Ask children to discuss how the language for the newspaper report differs from the story style of writing. (**previewing**)

During reading

- Ask the children to read Chapters 1–3.
- Ask them to look out for how Ant behaves in these chapters.

After reading

Returning to the text

- Ask the children:
- What is 'WOW!'? (**recall**)
- Why were the children going to 'WOW!'? (**recall**)
- What did you notice about Ant's behaviour? (**deducing, inferring and drawing conclusions**)

Building comprehension

- Ask the children, in turn, to say what they think happened to Ant when he briefly disappeared. What does the group think about each suggestion? How might Ant's behaviour affect the storyline later? (**deducing, inferring and drawing conclusions**)
- On page 14, why has the author commented that K J Sparkling is shorter and rounder than the children expected? How might this be significant to the rest of the story? (**predicting**)

· >

Building fluency

- Ask the children to reread pages 2–3 as if they are a TV reporter.

Building vocabulary

- Ask the children to choose one new word that they like from Chapters 1–3. Then bring the children together and play the echo game together (take it in turns to repeat the word around the group). Ask the children to add the new words to the *Vocabulary detectives* Photocopy Master.

> **Assessment point**
>
> Can the children identify clues in the text that may impact on the future storyline?
> Can they reflect on other people's ideas?
> Can children use evidence from the text and their own inferences to gain understanding about the characters? AF2/3

Session 2 (Chapters 4–6)

 Before reading

To activate prior knowledge and encourage prediction

- Ask the children to recall the significant events that have happened so far. Which events are likely to have the most significant impact on the storyline? Look at the title of Chapter 4 – *Another Arrival*. Who might this be? (**activating prior knowledge, predicting**)

During reading

- Ask the children to read Chapters 4–6.
- As they read, ask them to look out for how some of the key events earlier in the story are now explained.
- If you have not already done so, ask the children what to do if they encounter a difficult word, modelling with an example from the book if necessary, e.g. *autograph* (p31).

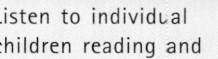
Assessment point

Listen to individual children reading and make ongoing assessments on their decoding, sight vocabulary, approaches to tackling new words and their reading fluency. **AF1**

•••➤

 After reading

Returning to the text

- Ask the children:
  - What device does the author use to show that the children have gone back in time? (Italics)
  - How does the real K J Sparkling compare with the impostor? (**personal response**)
  - Do you know any other stories in which it is the mum who saves the day?

Building comprehension

- Ask the children, in pairs, to take on the roles of the real K J Sparkling and the impostor. Ask them to assume a freeze frame position of the first time the two characters meet. (**visualizing**)
- Now ask the children to carry out a short role play imagining that they are the two women meeting for the first time. What might they say or think? (**empathizing**)

Assessment point

Can the children continue to use evidence from the text to gain understanding of the characters? **AF2/3**

•••➤

Session 3 (Chapters 7–8)

 Before reading

To activate prior knowledge and encourage prediction
- Recall what has happened in the story so far. What have been the high and low points of the story? (**recall, synthesizing, summarizing**)
- Can the children predict how Mrs X could be stopped? (**predicting**)

 During reading

- Ask the children to read Chapters 7–8.
- As they read, ask them to consider the emotions of the gang.
- If you have not already done so, ask the children what to do if they encounter a difficult word, modelling with an example from the book if necessary, e.g. *flabbergasted* (p.38).

 After reading

Returning to the text
- Ask the children:
  - Who took charge of the situation? Is this the character that you thought would take charge? What do we know about Max's character that would make us think he would take charge? (**recall, deducing, inferring and drawing conclusions**)
  - Why do you think the author decides that it is Max's mum that comes to the rescue? (**deducing, inferring and drawing conclusions**)

· ·>

Assessment point
Can the children interrogate the text to answer questions and make deductions about the story? **AF2/3**

Building comprehension

- Ask the children, as a group, to create a freeze frame image of the scene on the roof as Mrs X reveals her jet pack. Encourage them to think of body positions and where they might be in relation to other children. Encourage them to express their character's feelings through their facial expression and body language. (**visualizing**)

··························>

Assessment point

Have the children formed an accurate picture in their minds of the characters' feelings? AF2/3

- Encourage the children to reflect on and discuss the events in previous chapters that they thought would impact on the storyline. Did they predict the ones that would be most important for the story? (**determining importance**)

··························>

Assessment point

Can children reflect on ideas that others contribute to the discussion? AF3

Building vocabulary

- Ask the children to add new words to their *Vocabulary detectives* Photocopy Master.

Follow-up activities

Writing activities

- Use the *Dr X and Mrs X said...* Photocopy Master to write some possible dialogue between Dr X and his mum whilst they sit in jail. (**short writing task**)
- Children could write a new story in which a mum saves the day. (**longer writing task**)

Other literacy activities

- Use the *Comic strip writing frame* Photocopy Master to make a comic strip of the day's main events in *The WOW! Award*.

Cross-curricular and thematic opportunities

- Have an award ceremony in class or school to build children's self-esteem. (**PSHE**)
- Publish news reports. (**ICT**)
- Explore the history of newspapers and magazines. (**History**)

WOW!

BY ALEX LANE

About this book

This book is in the style of a magazine that features special guest authors Ant, Max, Cat and Tiger.

You will need

- *Book review* Photocopy Master, *Teaching Handbook* for Year 4/P5
- *Our favourite books* Photocopy Master, *Teaching Handbook* for Year 4/P5

	Literacy Framework objective	Target and assessment focus
Speaking, listening, group interaction and drama	○ Offer reasons and evidence for their views, considering alternative opinions 1.1	○ We can express personal preferences and give reasons for them **AF6**
Reading	○ Use knowledge of different organizational features of texts to find information effectively **7.3** ○ Read different genres and experiment with other types of text **8.1**	○ We can read more efficiently by understanding organizational features of non-fiction texts, including the layout of a page or spread **AF4** ○ We can recognize the language styles an author uses for different genres **AF5**

The following notes provide a structure for up to three guided/group reading sessions. They are intended to be used flexibly; you may choose to focus on all three sessions or you could focus on one session and have the children read the rest of the book independently.

In Session 1, children will read pages 2–19. In Session 2, they will read pages 30–31. In Session 3, children will read pages 20–29, 32–40. Sections not read during guided/group reading sessions should be read independently.

Session 1 (Pages 2–11, 14–19)

 Before reading

To activate prior knowledge and encourage prediction

- Ask the children what they notice about this book. Scan through the pages. How is it different from all the others in the series? (**previewing**)
- Have the children ever read a magazine or comic? (**activating prior knowledge**)
- Read the *Hero Snap Shots* on pages 2–3 together. What new information do the children discover about the main characters? (**activating and building prior knowledge**)

To engage readers and support fluent reading

- Turn to pages 4–7 and look at the comic strip of the defeat of Dr X. Does the strip tell the same version of events that the children remember?

To introduce new vocabulary

- Ask the children to scan through the magazine, collect any new or unfamiliar words, then create a blank 'magazine' for them to add the words to. During their independent reading activities they can begin to find the definitions for these words.

During reading

- Ask each child to read a different double page spread from pages 2–11 or pages 14–19. Explain that each of these spreads represents a different genre or style of writing.
- As they read, ask them to notice what features their pages have. Encourage them to use their understanding of the style to retrieve and read information more efficiently.

 After reading

Returning to the text

- Ask the children to explain what particular genre their double page spread was an example of.
- How did it compare with other spreads that the rest of the group have read?
- Did they like the style and genre or would they prefer to read information in a different way? (**personal response**)
- How did the writer's use of language change between the different styles?

· ·>

Building comprehension

- Ask children to summarize their double page spread to the rest of the group using no more than 20 words. (**summarizing**)
- Choose two of the children's favourite double page spreads. Appoint two children to act as advocates for each page and put forward all their reasons for that spread to be chosen as the best spread. Invite other children to argue the case within a debate style forum. At the end, ask each child to vote for the best spread. (**questioning, determining importance, drawing conclusions, personal response**)

· ·>

> **Assessment point**
>
> - Do the children use the organizational features of non-fiction texts to read more efficiently and responsively? **AF4**
> - Can the children comment on the writers' use of language? **AF5**

> **Assessment point**
>
> Can the children express personal preferences and consider other people's opinions? **AF6**

Session 2 (Pages 30–31)

Before reading

- For this session to be successful, it would be helpful if children have read one or more of the books that are reviewed in *Cat and Tiger's book review* on pages 30–31.

To activate prior knowledge and encourage prediction

- Discuss the children's favourite books. What type of books do they enjoy and why? Do they prefer fiction or non-fiction? What different types of media do they enjoy reading? e.g. magazines, newspapers, information books. (**personal response, activating and building prior knowledge**)
- Why do they think people write book reviews? (**deducing, inferring and drawing conclusions**)

During reading

- Ask the children to read pages 30–31.
- As they read, ask them to look for clues that these reviews were meant to be written by children rather than adults.
- If you have not already done so, ask the children what to do if they encounter a difficult word, modelling with an example from the book if necessary, e.g. *hypnotize* (p.30).

> **Assessment point**
>
> Listen to individual children reading and make ongoing assessments on their decoding, sight vocabulary, approaches to tackling new words and their reading fluency. AF1

After reading

Returning to the text

- Ask the children:
  - What clues are there to show that these reviews were written by Tiger and Cat? (**deducing, inferring and drawing conclusions**)
  - What did you notice about the language and vocabulary?
  - How helpful are the reviews? (**personal response, including adopting a critical stance**)

○ Are there any other points that should be included to help you to decide whether to read the books? (**determining importance**)

Building comprehension

● Ask the children which book was the most popular and how they know.

● If there are any books that the children have read, how do the reviews compare with their opinions about them?

● How else could the information have been presented to make it easier to decide which was the best book? (**visualizing**)

● What other information would they like to know about one of the books? (**questioning**)

Session 3 (Pages 20–29, 32–40)

 Before reading

To engage readers

● Explain that the children will choose a spread they would like to read from the rest of the book. What styles of writing and presentation do they prefer? Help the children to make a decision about which page they would like to read.

 During reading

● Ask the children to read their chosen spread.

● As they read, ask them to evaluate the spread, looking out for ways the information is presented in terms of layout.

 After reading

Returning to the text

● Ask the children:

○ What did you like about the page you chose? What didn't you like about it? (**personal response, including adopting a critical stance**)

○ Is there a different page that you wish you had chosen? Why?

Assessment point

Can the children give their opinions about their chosen page? AF6

. . . . ➤

Building comprehension

◉ Ask the children to create their own review of this book to be included in a class magazine. What information would they put in it? (**visualizing**)

◉ Are there any sections from *Wow! Special Edition* that the children think were more successful than others? Are there any that were less successful than others? (**personal response, including adopting a critical stance**)

Follow-up activities

Writing activities

◉ Children could write their own book review, using the *Book review* Photocopy Master. (**short writing task**)

◉ Children could create a piece of writing from a different point of view similar to the style of Mrs X's piece on page 27 – *My Son is Innocent*. (**longer writing task**)

◉ Write a class magazine. (**longer writing task**)

Cross-curricular and thematic opportunities

◉ Carry out a class survey to find out what the children's favourite books are, using the *Our favourite books* Photocopy Master. (**Maths**)

◉ Carry out science investigations and write reports for the class magazine. (**Science**)

◉ Design a recipe for the class magazine. (**DT**)

◉ Make your own 'X Marks the Spot' page (see pages 36–37). (**Geography**)

◉ Create an 'Agony Ant' column and let children send in their problems for Ant to help them solve. (**PSHE**)

Micro Man Makes Big News

BY EMMA LYNCH

About this book

This book looks at journalistic writing, by using the example of Willard Wigan – an artist who makes micro sculptures. It shows how journalists present information in different ways.

You will need

- *What do we know about Willard?* Photocopy Master, *Teaching Handbook* for Year 4/P5
- *Direct and reported speech* Photocopy Master, *Teaching Handbook* for Year 4/P5
- Range of magazines, newspapers and web-based journalistic reports on different people
- Ball bearings

	Literacy Framework objective	Target and assessment focus
Speaking, listening, group interaction and drama	○ Respond appropriately to the contributions of others in the light of differing viewpoints 1.2	○ We can debate issues and reach a decision, listening to and responding to different views **AF2**
Reading	○ Use knowledge of different organizational features of texts to find information effectively 7.3 ○ Read extensively ... genres and experiment with other types of text 8.1	○ We can locate information to support our views **AF2/3** ○ We can read and recognize a range of genres and give our preferences **AF4**

The following notes provide a structure for up to three guided/group reading sessions. They are intended to be used flexibly; you may choose to focus on all three sessions or you could focus on one session and have the children read the rest of the book independently. In Session 1, children will read pages 2–9. Children will then need to read pages 10–13 independently. In Session 2, they will read pages 14–25. In Session 3, children will read pages 26–30.

Session 1 (Pages 2–9)

 Before reading

To activate prior knowledge and encourage prediction

- Read the title of the book to the children. Ask them to imagine what the book might be about. (**predicting**)
- Show children a range of magazine, newspaper and website reports on different people to browse through and discuss. Ask them to list the different features used in each report to include on a central display on journalism. (**activating and building prior knowledge**)

To engage readers

- Discuss different people who have inspired the children. You might like to visit a newspaper office or invite a journalist into the school to talk to the children. (**personal response**)

To introduce new vocabulary

- Ask the children to look through the book and collect all the words that are in bold. Help them to decode these words, and then turn to the glossary to find out the meanings of the words.

 During reading

- Ask the children to read to the end of page 9.
- As they read ask them to look out for journalistic words such as *broadcast, issues* (p.3), *headlines* (p.5), *reported speech, quotes* (p.6).

- If you have not already done so, ask the children what to do if they encounter a difficult word, modelling with an example from the book if necessary. Remind them of the more challenging vocabulary which you looked at before reading the book.

Assessment point

Listen to individual children reading and make ongoing assessments on their decoding, sight vocabulary, approaches to tackling new words and their reading fluency. **AF1**

 After reading

Returning to the text

- Ask the children:
  - What have you learned about Willard Wigan so far? (**recall**)
  - What significant moment led Willard into this unusual career? (**recall, determining importance**)
- Encourage the children to write down information they have discovered about Willard Wigan on the *What do we know about Willard?* Photocopy Master.
- Look at pages 8 and 9. Which style do the children prefer – the simple webpage recount or the comic strip? Why? (**personal response**)

Assessment point

Can the children express their opinions about the presentation and style of the text? **AF4**

Building comprehension

- Ask the children to pretend to be a reporter and generate questions that they might like to ask Willard Wigan. Ensure they form closed and open questions to obtain specific and more in-depth information. (**questioning**)
- Then, with one child acting as Willard, give the other children an opportunity to ask their questions, encouraging 'Willard' to use the text to back up some answers.
- Before Session 2, ask the children to read pages 10–13 independently.

Before reading

To activate prior knowledge and engage the reader

- Review the questions that the children developed in the previous session. Is there one thing that they really want to find out about Willard Wigan and his work? Discuss what other information they found out when they read the recount on pages 10–13 independently. Do they now have any other questions? (**recall, questioning**)

 During reading

- Ask the children to read pages 14–25.
- As they read, ask them to think about whether the questions that are asked are similar to the ones they created.

 After reading

Returning to the text

- Ask the children:
  - What have you found out about Willard Wigan? (**recall**)
  - How effective do you think the interviewer's questions were? (**determining importance, adopting a critical stance**)
  - What other questions would you have liked to ask Willard? (**questioning, personal response**)

Building comprehension

- Ask the children to consider how Willard Wigan feels about his schooling. (**empathizing**)

Assessment point

Were the children able to find information in the text to back up their answers? **AF2/AF3**

- Provide each child with a ball bearing (or similar object) and ask them to see if they can balance it on their finger for one minute. How does it feel? Can they imagine how difficult it must have been for Willard to balance it for three hours? What does this tell us about Willard's character? (**empathizing, deducing, inferring and drawing conclusions**)

Building fluency

- Ask the children, in pairs, to reread pages 14–24 as if they are carrying out the interview between the reporter and Willard Wigan.

Session 3 (Pages 26–30)

 Before reading

To engage the reader

- Look at the title of this section: *Different points of view*. What different points of view might exist about Willard Wigan? e.g. his teachers' opinions of him, his mother's opinion, etc. Explain to the children that some people do not like Willard Wigan's sculptures. How do the children feel about this? (**personal response**)

 During reading

- Ask the children to read pages 26–30.
- As they read, ask them to think about whether they agree with the different points of view. (**personal response**)

 After reading

Returning to the text

- Ask the children which statements or points of view they agreed with. What do they feel about Willard's work? (**personal response**)

Building comprehension

- Encourage the children to debate Willard's work. Can they understand other people's points of view? (**empathizing, personal response, including adopting a critical stance**)

······································>

- Ask the children to work in a group to review the book. Which style of reporting did they feel was most successful? (**personal response, including adopting a critical stance**)

Building vocabulary

- Look at the word *microscope* (p.3). Focus on the prefix 'micro' and discuss what this means. Model how this prefix plus the suffix forms the word. How many different words can children make with 'micro'?

Follow-up activities

Writing activities

- Write headlines that capture people's attention for events that are happening in the world or at school. (**short writing task**)
- Ask the children to become journalists. Help them to find someone that they think would make an interesting subject for a newspaper or magazine report. Allow them to research the subject, carry out interviews and then decide how they will present the information. (**longer writing task**)

Other literacy activities

- Search the text to find examples of direct and reported speech and list them on the *Direct and reported speech* Photocopy Master.

Cross-curricular and thematic opportunities

- Discuss the question: How would you feel if you lost something you had spent a month working on? (**PSHE**)
- Make miniature sculptures and research the micro-sculptors Hagop Sandaljian and Nikolai Syadristy. (**Art and design**)
- Explore magnification. (**Maths**)
- Use microscopes and hand lenses to study objects. (**Science**)

The Big Story

BY DOMINIC BARKER

About this book

This book tells the story of Jack, who is desperate to become a reporter. On his quest to have a story printed he comes across a scandal on his own doorstep.

You will need

- *Character profile* Photocopy Master, *Teaching Handbook* for Year 4/P5
- *UltraGym* Photocopy Master, *Teaching Handbook* for Year 4/P5
- Range of tabloid, broadsheet and local newspapers (including 'First News')

	Literacy Framework objective	Target and assessment focus
Speaking, listening, group interaction and drama	○ Offer reasons and evidence for their views, considering alternative opinions 1.1	○ We can use visual and written evidence to infer what is not said explicitly in the text **AF2/3**
Reading	○ Deduce characters' reasons for behaviour from their actions 7.2	○ We can talk about why characters behave in different ways **AF3**
	○ Interrogate texts to deepen and clarify understanding and response 8.2	○ We can show some understanding of a writer's viewpoint (e.g. whose side the writer seems to be on) **AF6**

The following notes provide a structure for up to three guided/group reading sessions. They are intended to be used flexibly; you may choose to focus on all three sessions or you could focus on one session and have the children read the rest of the book independently.

In Session 1, children will read Chapters 1–3. In Session 2, they will read Chapters 4–5. Children will then need to read Chapters 6–7 independently prior to Session 3. In Session 3, children will read Chapters 8–11.

Session 1 (Chapters 1–3)

 Before reading

To activate prior knowledge and encourage prediction

- Talk to the children about their aspirations. What would they like to be when they are older? Who or what has inspired them to want to do that role? Explain that *The Big Story* is all about a young boy who desperately wants to be a news reporter. What do children understand about how a newspaper is created? What different roles are needed to create a newspaper? (**activating prior knowledge**)

- Hand out any newspapers you may have to show examples of the differences between broadsheet, tabloid and local newspapers. You might also like to include 'First News' (a newspaper for children). Talk to children about the differences, ideally choosing a story that has been reported in each of the papers. Discuss how tabloids often exaggerate facts to make the story more exciting whilst the journalism in broadsheets is of a higher quality. You may like to introduce bias at this point if you are working with a particularly able group.

> **Assessment point**
>
> Can the children identify the different writing styles and viewpoints in each of the papers? AF6

· ·➔

During reading

- Ask the children to read Chapters 1–3. You might want to remind them of some of the journalistic vocabulary that they have collected if they have read other books in this cluster.

- As they read, ask them to think about the characteristics of the people in the story so far: Jack Rico, Jack's friend Molly, Veronica – the secretary at *The Norton Gazette* and Mr Richardson the editor.

After reading

Returning to the text

- Ask the children what they have deduced about the characters so far. Encourage them to back up their opinions with reference to the text. (**deducing, inferring and drawing conclusions**)

- How could Jack have asked Molly more sensitively about how she feels about the closure of the pool? (**empathizing**)

································>

- What do children notice about the language and style of the report on page 6? What tense is it written in?

> **Assessment point**
>
> Can the children draw conclusions about the characters from their behaviour and what they say? **AF3**

Building comprehension

- In pairs, ask one child to take on the role of Molly Green and the other to take on the role of Jack Rico. Invite 'Jack' to interview 'Molly' to find out how she really feels about the closure of the swimming pool. (**questioning, empathizing**)

- Focus on the language and style of the 'interview' on page 8. What impact do the children think this style of writing has on the reader? Point out how the story has been written in the present tense to try to imitate a news reporting style. (**deducing, inferring and drawing conclusions**)

- Ask the children to complete character profiles for Jack, Molly, Veronica and Mr Richardson, using the *Character profile* Photocopy Master.

Chapter 8

Day: Wednesday
Time: 5:40 pm
Location: Norton Park

Dave Howard charges down the main street, tightly clutching his backpack to his chest. He turns left at some traffic lights and then right soon after. He walks faster and faster, holding the backpack tighter and tighter. He's looking at everybody. After all, he's carrying a lot of money and someone might be a thief.

It makes it hard for Jack to follow him. He has to duck behind a wall, then hide behind a tree, then pretend to be bending over tying his laces.

When he looks up, there's no sign of Howard. Jack can't believe he's lost him. This could be his last chance to find out what's happening. He dashes down the street, his head darting frantically from side to side. Just in time, he spots Howard slipping into Norton Park. Jack's not going to lose him again. He sprints into the park.

Session 2 (Chapters 4–5)

 Before reading

To activate prior knowledge and engage the reader

- Review the story so far. Who are the main characters? What have been the key events so far? (**activating prior knowledge, determining importance**)

- Take a picture walk through pages 16–28 to see if the children can predict what might happen next. (**previewing, predicting**)

- Look at the picture of Mr Howard on page 19. What can the children deduce about his character using clues from the picture? (**deducing, inferring and drawing conclusions, visualizing**)

> **Assessment point**
>
> Can the children use visual evidence to infer what is not said explicitly in the text and back up their reasons? AF3

. . . . >

 During reading

- Ask the children to read Chapters 4–5.

- As they read, ask them to notice the language that the author uses to give more clues about Mr Howard's personality.

- If you have not already done so, ask the children what to do if they encounter a difficult word, modelling with an example from the book if necessary.

> **Assessment point**
>
> Listen to individual children reading and make ongoing assessments on their decoding, sight vocabulary, approaches to tackling new words and their reading fluency. AF1

. . . . >

 After reading

Returning to the text

- Mr Howard says that he wants everyone to "think of me as a friend" (p.19). Ask the children whether they would want to be friends with him. (**deducing, inferring and drawing conclusions**)

Building comprehension

- Ask the children to reread the news report on page 24. What do they notice about it? What lies can they find in the report? Can the children suggest reasons why the report might be filled with lies and exaggerations? (**deducing, inferring and drawing conclusions**)

- Invite the children, in pairs, to carry out a short role play, imagining that they are Jack and Molly reading the newspaper article. How would they react? What might they say? (**empathizing**)

Assessment point

Can the children deduce what characters might say, based on their knowledge of the characters? AF3

· ·>

- Before Session 3, ask the children to read Chapters 6–7 independently.

Session 3 (Chapters 8–11)

 Before reading

To activate prior knowledge and engage the reader

- Ask the children what happened in Chapters 6–7. Why do they think the previous ten people became members of UltraGym? (**recall**)
- How might the news article (back on page 24) have influenced people to join the gym? (**deducing, inferring and drawing conclusions**)

 During reading

- Ask the children to read Chapters 8–11.
- As they read, ask them to look out for clues that might explain what has *really* been going on and why the pool had been closed.
- If you have not already done so, ask the children what to do if they encounter a difficult word, modelling with an example from the book if necessary.

Assessment point

Listen to individual children reading and make ongoing assessments on their decoding, sight vocabulary, approaches to tackling new words and their reading fluency. AF1

· ·>

 After reading

Returning to the text

- Ask the children:
  o Were Dave Howard and Arthur Pribit really duck watchers? (**deducing, inferring and drawing conclusions**)

- How was Veronica giving the tape recorder to Jack in an earlier chapter important for the story later on? (**drawing conclusions**)
- Can the children say how important Veronica is to the story? Why? (**determining importance**)
- Why was Mr Richardson so grovelling to Jack at the end? (**deducing, inferring and drawing conclusions**)

Building comprehension

- Ask the children, in small groups, to use the evidence in the story and their understanding of the characters, to discuss an explanation of what had been going on. The children could write their findings and predictions as a newspaper report. (**deducing, inferring and drawing conclusions, determining importance, synthesizing**)

> **Assessment point**
>
> Were the children able to listen and respond to each other's views about happenings in the story that haven't been explicitly stated? Were they able to locate information to support their views? AF2/3

- Read page 52 with the children and compare the story Jack wrote with their own predictions about what had happened. (**synthesizing**)

Follow-up activities

Writing activities

- Invite the children to create newspaper headlines for school, local and world events. (**short writing task**).
- Ask the children to write a news report of a sports activity at school. (**longer writing task**)

Cross-curricular and thematic opportunities

- Publish some newspaper reports. (**ICT**)
- Take part or watch sporting events and then write reports about them. (**PE**)
- Design a poster to advertise UltraGym using the *UltraGym* Photocopy Master. (**Art and design**)

Making a Splash

BY CHLOE RHODES

About this book

This book shows how the news of a stranded whale in the River Thames was reported in different ways using television, newspapers and the Internet.

You will need

- *Subject and journalistic words* Photocopy Master, *Teaching Handbook* for Year 4/P5

	Literacy Framework objective	Target and assessment focus
Speaking, listening, group interaction and drama	○ Offer reasons and evidence for their views, considering alternative opinions 1.1 ○ Respond appropriately to the contributions of others in the light of differing viewpoints 1.2	○ We can debate issues and reach a decision, listening to and responding to different views **AF2/3**
Reading	○ Use knowledge of different organizaional features of texts to find information effectively 7.3 ○ Identify and summarize evidence from a text to support a hypothesis 7.1 ○ Read extensively ... genres and experiment with other types of texts 8.1	○ We can locate information efficiently and use it to support our ideas **AF2** ○ We can read and recognize a range of genres including mixed genre texts **AF4**

The following notes provide a structure for up to three guided/group reading sessions. They are intended to be used flexibly; you may choose to focus on all three sessions or you could focus on one session and have the children read the rest of the book independently.

In Session 1, children will read pages 2–11. In Session 2, they will choose a section from pages 12–17. In Session 3, children will read pages 18–25. Sections not read during guided/group reading sessions should be read independently.

Session 1 (Pages 2–11)

 Before reading

To activate prior knowledge and encourage prediction

● Talk to the children about how a bottle-nose whale was discovered swimming in the Thames. Talk to them about why this is unusual and how a huge rescue was mounted to try to save the whale. You may or may not choose to reveal that the rescue was unsuccessful at this point. (**previewing**)

To introduce new vocabulary

● Explain the vocabulary in this book: technical vocabulary linked to news, and subject-specific vocabulary related to whales. Give the children the *Subject and journalistic words* Photocopy Master to collect vocabulary and write their definitions.

 During reading

● Ask the children to read pages 2–11.
● As they read, ask them to notice the different presentational features.
● If you have not already done so, ask the children what to do if they encounter a difficult word, modelling with an example from the book if necessary, e.g. *estuary* (p.11).

· ·>

Assessment point
Listen to individual children reading and make ongoing assessments on their decoding, sight vocabulary, approaches to tackling new words and their reading fluency. **AF1**

 **After reading**

Returning to the text

- Briefly discuss the children's immediate thoughts about the whale.
- Which double-page spread interested the children most? Can they give reasons why? Did the way the information was presented influence their decision? (**personal response, including adopting a critical stance**)

· >

- Ask all children to use the index to locate in the text the answers to these questions:
  - Who are the Divers Marine Life Rescue?
  - How does a news agency become involved in reporting?

Building comprehension

- Ask the children to make brief notes about the information in the text using three bullet points under these headings: 'What happened to the whale?'; 'How can a reporter find out the facts?' (**synthesizing, inferring, deducing, summarizing**)
- Ask the children to formulate a hypothesis to explain how the whale ended up in the River Thames. (**synthesizing**)

Building vocabulary

- Look at the word *conservation* (p.10). Focus on the core word 'conserve' and discuss what this means. Model how this core word, plus its suffix, forms the word. How many different words can children make from the word 'conserve'?

Session 2 (Pages 12–17)

To activate prior knowledge and engage the reader

- Recap what the children have read so far. (**recall**)
- Explain that they will choose whether to focus on TV news reporting (pages 12–13), online news reporting (pages 14–15) or newspaper reporting (pages 16–17). Discuss how the three forms might differ in the way they create the news. Which do they prefer? (**personal response**)

During reading

- Ask the children to read their chosen section from pages 12–17.
- As they read, ask them to note down key features of their chosen media form.

 After reading

Returning to the text

- Talk to the children about the main features of their chosen spread. Encourage them to talk about the good and bad points of the news form. (**adopting a critical response**)

> **Assessment point**
>
> Can the children listen, respond and agree on the good and bad points of each form of news reporting? AF2/3

· ·>

Building comprehension

- Ask the children as a group to discuss the different news forms. Encourage the children to draw conclusions about how they prefer to receive their news and why. (**personal response**)

Session 3 (Pages 18–25)

 Before reading

To activate prior knowledge and engage the reader

- Recap the information that the children have found out so far.
- Can they predict how the whale might be rescued? (**predicting**)

 During reading

- Ask the children to read pages 18–25.
- Ask them to draw conclusions about how well the rescue is going.

 **After reading**

Returning to the text

- Ask the children how they feel after having read the conclusion to the story of the whale. (**personal respons**e)
- Ask them to review the different genres. Which style was the most accessible to read? (**adopting a critical stance**)

··>

Building comprehension

> **Assessment point**
>
> Can the children read and recognize a range of genres including mixed genre texts? **AF4**

- Ask the children to name some of the different ways that people tried to save the whale. (**recall**)
- How did the newspaper and TV crews gain the public's help? Why are news broadcasts and appeals good ways to do this? (**deducing, inferring and drawing conclusions**)
- Ask each pair of children to select a preferred form of news reporting: television, newspaper or the Internet. Ask one child to argue for its use, while the other argues against its use. Encourage the children to use their notes to help them. (**determining importance, synthesizing**)

··>

> **Assessment point**
>
> Were the children able to debate the topic, listening and responding to each other's views? **AF2/3**

Follow-up activities

Writing activities

- Invite the children to write news flashes for significant events. (**short writing task**)
- Ask them to report on a significant or made-up event and decide whether to report it as a TV, newspaper, or Internet news report. (**longer writing task**)

Other literacy activities

- Set up a debate to discuss whether everything was done correctly to save the whale. (**speaking and listening**)

Cross-curricular and thematic opportunities

- Look at the conservation of habitats and living things. (**Science**)
- Map the migration routes of whales. (**Geography**)
- Explore web-based newspapers. Use instant messaging or similar to create a news flash. (**ICT**)